What is Consent? Why is it Important? And Other Big Questions

Louise Spilsbury & Yas Necati

Published in paperback in Great Britain in 2018 by Wayland

Copyright © Hodder and Stoughton, 2017

ISBN: 978 1 5263 0092 8

10 9 8 7 6 5 4 3 2 1

Printed in China

Wayland
An imprint of
Hachette Children's Group
Part of Hodder & Stoughton
Carmelite House
50 Victoria Embankment
London EC4Y 0DZ

An Hachette UK Company
www.hachette.co.uk
www.hachettechildrens.co.uk

Editor: Elizabeth Brent
Designer: Grant Kempster
Cover design: Oli Frape

Picture acknowledgements: All images courtesy of Shutterstock.com, except: p34 Getty Images/Science Photo Library; p39 stocklight/Shutterstock.com

Contents

Introducing CONSENT

Have you ever agreed to do something you didn't really want to do? Do you say yes sometimes when you're really thinking no? Do you sometimes try to convince other people to do things even when you know they don't want to? The aim of this book is to get everyone thinking and talking about the issue of consent. How does it work? Why does it matter?

You may have heard the word consent before and wondered what it means. Perhaps you heard it during a marriage service, when a couple declares they consent to marry one another. Or perhaps you have had to ask for a parent's consent to be allowed to access a website. The idea of consent might seem simple enough, but some people get confused about whether or not someone has actually given consent, or when and how it is given. What consent really means, and why it matters so much, can be complicated.

"*Consent is not the absence of a no; it is the presence of a yes.*"

Erin Riordan, writer

We all grow up learning that if someone says 'no,' then you need to listen to them. No means no. This is a very important part of consent, but it is normally as far as any discussion about it goes and that's a shame as it's not the whole story. It sometimes leaves people thinking that so long as someone doesn't say no, that means they have given their consent. In fact, consent is more complicated than that.

How the BOOK WORKS

In this book, we'll look at what the word consent really means and why it is so important.

We'll look at what consent means for you and how to tell people whether or not you consent, how to communicate your feelings, and how to deal with people who try to tease or pressurise you into doing something you don't want to do. We'll also look at how to recognise when other people don't give their consent, and at some of the specific areas where consent has powerful impacts, such as sexual consent, medical consent and consenting in the online world. We'll tackle some big questions such as 'When is consent not really consent?' and 'What can we do when consent is abused?'.

Some people from the worlds of media, politics, campaigning and medicine have also written about what consent means and how it affects their and our lives. These interviews are spread throughout the book. There are quotes saying interesting and important things about consent and there are some questions to get you thinking about the issues surrounding consent as you read the book.

What is CONSENT?

The dictionary definition of consent is 'to give permission for something to happen'. People can give or refuse consent in a whole range of situations. So, if someone asks to borrow your bike and you say yes, you give them consent to use it. If a girl asks a boy to be her boyfriend and he says no, he is refusing to consent to a relationship with her.

> **_Consent is vital. It's always a person's right to decide what they want to happen to them. It's never okay to try to make someone do something that they don't want to do._**
> Pavan Amara, campaigner

The idea of consent seems simple enough, but in reality it can be quite complicated. To explain what consent means, people often use the idea of 'enthusiastic consent'. This tells us that consent is something active. Consent means someone is freely choosing to say 'yes'. They are giving their consent willingly and happily and in full knowledge of what that decision means for them. So, if someone ends up giving their consent because they have been pressured into it, or they feel bad about refusing, that's not consent. If someone doesn't really understand what it means to give their consent or they are scared to refuse consent, it does not count as consent. Consent not freely given is not being given at all, even if someone says yes.

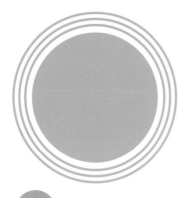

Consent plays a part in big decisions, such as whether someone chooses to have a hospital operation or not, or whether they want to get married or not. Consent is also an important part of our everyday lives, and comes into play with almost every interaction we make. When you get on the bus, you are consenting to be driven to your chosen destination by the bus driver. When you pay for something in a shop, you are consenting to exchange your money for whatever you're buying.

In many situations, we give consent easily, but in some we might have to think about our decision more, or refuse consent. It's important for other people to respect your right to refuse consent, just as it's important for you to respect other people's right to do the same.

Words to do with CONSENT

Voluntary

For consent to be valid, it must be voluntary. The decision must be made by the person giving consent, and must not be influenced by pressure from friends, family or others.

Informed

To be able to consent to something, a person must know the benefits and risks of their decision, including what might happen if they do or don't give consent.

Capacity

For a person to be capable of giving consent, they must be able to understand the information given to them, so they can use it to make an informed decision about whether or not to consent. That's why someone cannot give their consent to do something if they are asleep, unconscious or drunk, or do not have the mental capacity to make an informed decision.

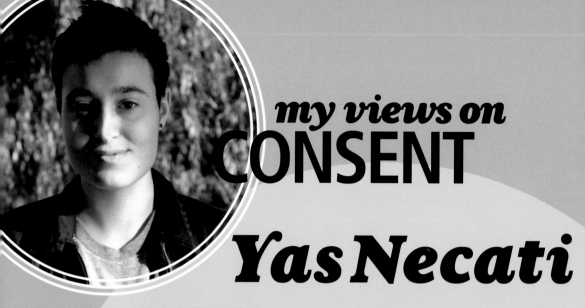

my views on
CONSENT

Yas Necati

YAS NECATI left school feeling like she hadn't been taught enough about consent. She now campaigns to get consent on the school curriculum, and for better sex and relationships education.

ON HER OWN PERSONAL *boundaries*

I feel like personal boundaries are different for everyone. For example, I don't mind giving high fives to people I don't know very well, but somebody else might not like that. There are things that I'm okay with, and things that I'm not okay with. I'm quite a small person, and I really don't like it when taller people lean or stand over me. Sometimes when the train is really busy, I end up standing under someone's armpit as they lean over me to reach the overhead hand rail. I don't like that because I feel like it's invading my personal space (it can also sometimes be a bit smelly!). Somebody else might not mind it though. I think it's up to each person to know their personal boundaries, and what they do and don't like. It's important to remember that you need to decide for yourself what makes you feel comfortable, and what doesn't.

THINK ABOUT

Can you think of times you have consented to something and it's made you feel happy?

Can you think of times you have consented to something just to make another person happy?

DO PERSONAL BOUNDARIES *change?*

Our own personal boundaries can change in different situations, depending on how well we know a person and how comfortable we feel being close to them. I wouldn't be happy if a stranger or someone I wasn't very close to just came up to me and hugged me without asking first. Even if they did ask, I might say no because I didn't feel very comfortable. However, if my friend who I always hugged, hugged me without asking first, most of the time I would be okay with this. Hugs from friends usually make me feel happy and loved and I really enjoy them.

How about if you don't want a hug from a friend?

> **It's up to each person to know their personal boundaries, and what they do and don't like.**

Sometimes I might not feel like a hug, or someone hugging me might make me feel uncomfortable, even if I'm close to them and we've hugged lots of times before. Whoever the person is, and no matter how close you are, if something makes you feel uncomfortable, then you don't have to do it. If someone is a good friend, they will understand, because they won't want to do anything that makes you unhappy.

OWNING YOUR *body*

Always remember that your body is yours and it's up to you how you want to interact with other people. Nobody can know what does and doesn't feel right for you, apart from you. So trust yourself when you feel uncomfortable, and trust yourself when you feel happy. You will always know best what's right for you.

my views on
CONSENT

Louise Spilsbury

LOUISE SPILSBURY has been an author for over 20 years and has written more than 200 books on a wide range of topics, from art to alligators, and zips to zoos, but she has a special interest in feminism.

WHY IS THE ISSUE OF CONSENT *important?*

I'm fascinated by the issue of consent. Something that seems so straightforward but really isn't. Consent for me is bound up with ideas of self-esteem and confidence. In knowing yourself and knowing that it is absolutely fine and right for people to say what they really want or don't want. When I was young, good girls were expected to be compliant and giving and to always think of other people's needs. I wish there had been more information and emphasis on the importance of consent while I was growing up.

THINK ABOUT

Do you think girls today are still expected to be nicer than boys? Why do you think that might be?

Do you think that is fair?

WHAT'S WRONG WITH *being nice?*

The problem with always being told to be nice is that too often it means girls and women are brought up thinking they can't be honest about their feelings. They make up reasons why they are not going to a party because it's not 'nice' to just say they don't want to go. They find it hard to tell someone they don't like something the other person likes. Too often girls are brought up to think that it's wrong to say or ask for what they want. This pressure comes from subtle messages that girls and women receive every day from people around them, and TV, films and other forms of the media. Basically, girls and women are taught to be nice rather than be honest about how they think and feel. This might suit some of the people around them, who get their own way more often than not, but it's not helping girls and women and it's not right or fair!

HOW CAN CONSENT *empower us?*

When we talk about how important consent is, what we are really saying is that every individual's feelings and desires matter. It is empowering for people to know that they have the right to put their feelings first. It's only when we know our feelings and needs are as important as anyone else's that we are able to negotiate choices and decisions fairly.

People need to know that they are entitled to decide what they do or consent to for themselves, and not be expected to make choices to please others. When people fully understand what consent means, and that to give consent you need to fully recognise, own and accept your feelings, we are giving women, and men, the confidence to freely speak up and defend what they believe in and to help them be proud of who they are.

> **"Girls and women are taught to be nice rather than be honest about how they think and feel."**

Recognising
CONSENT

There are lots of ways to tell when someone is giving their consent and they don't always include the word 'yes'. Learning how to recognise when people are giving enthusiastic consent is really important to ensure we are all genuinely happy with the choices we make, and it's really not that hard to do!

Enthusiastic consent

Someone giving an active, visible, undeniable yes to a question or request is enthusiastic consent. It's easy to spot enthusiastic consent. Think about asking for a hug – and we should always ask people if it's okay to hug or tickle them or hold their hand or otherwise enter their personal space. If you ask 'Can I have a hug goodbye?' that gives people the choice. If they give you clear and enthusiastic consent, they say and do something like 'Yes, I'd love a hug' or 'Yes, it's okay for you to hug me', while looking you in the eyes and opening their arms wide towards to you. If this is the sort of reaction you get, then it's okay to hug them. If an active, visible, undeniable 'yes' doesn't happen, then they shouldn't be touched. You accept and respect their choice and simply say 'No problem.'

READING *the signs*

A non-response is not the same thing as someone saying yes. If someone says nothing, they have not said yes enthusiastically. So, they have not given their consent. And sometimes people say yes when they really mean no. This could be because they don't want to upset the person asking for the hug, because they're not really sure if they want a hug, or any one of lots of other reasons. Even if someone says yes, we can tell they mean no by all the other signals they are giving off. When someone isn't being totally honest, experts think that more than half of their communication comes from their body language. Body language is the way we use postures or gestures to express our feelings: the way we stand, how we hold our arms and the different expressions on our face.

People give off clear signals when they are not happy or not being honest about how they feel. Are they frowning, looking away or looking at their feet? Do they have their arms crossed in front of their body in a defensive way? Do they freeze up when you try to hug them or do they pull their body away? These are all clear signs that someone is not giving enthusiastic consent. And anything other than enthusiastic consent is not consent.

55% of communication is body language, 38% is the tone of voice, and 7% is the actual words spoken.

7%
words spoken

38%
tone of voice

55%
body language

my views on CONSENT

David Bartlett

DAVID BARTLETT is the chief executive of the White Ribbon campaign, a charity that reaches out to men and boys to encourage them to challenge male violence against women and girls.

WHAT HAS GENDER GOT TO DO WITH *consent?*

From a very young age, boys often feel pressured to fit into certain gender roles about what it means to 'be a man'. Some of these gender roles can be positive, like protecting others and providing safety and security. But some of them can also be confusing or negative. For example boys are taught that they should always be in charge and not get pushed around by anyone – especially by a girl.

Boys are often expected to be the 'initiator' in romantic or sexual relationships. They can sometimes be too assertive or pushy because underneath it they're worried about rejection. It's hard to hear 'no'. But it's important to respect someone when they say they don't want to consent to something. You're still okay if someone says no to you. They're okay, and you're okay as well. So no can be good. Respecting when someone else says no is a sign of a healthy relationship.

> **❝ So no can be good. Respecting when someone else says no is a sign of a healthy relationship. ❞**

WHAT IF A BOY HAS HIS
consent breached?

***"It's important to respect someone when they say they don't want to consent to something."*

Boys are often given the message that they shouldn't show vulnerability or admit that they have problems. Sometimes boys might feel like they can't talk about their emotions or difficult things that have happened because of this. If someone disregards a boy's right to consent, he might stay silent and not share what has happened because he's scared of being judged. I'd want to reassure boys that they won't be judged. Everyone has a right to have their opinion respected.

Talking about how you're feeling shows strength and makes you stronger. The ability to be honest and work through things you might be struggling with is very strong. We are all just people and we all have problems sometimes. Boys aren't always taught that listening to your emotions is strong, but it is.

THINK ABOUT

Can you think of stereotypes about boys and girls?

How might these stereotypes affect the way we talk about consent?

Your BODY, *Your* CHOICE

Consent matters because everyone's opinion, feelings and wishes matter. It is about choice – what you choose to do or have done to you. Everyone has different personal boundaries, and the right to choose what happens to their body.

Personal boundaries are the rules a person has about the ways other people behave towards them. The rules define what they like and don't like or what feels good and what doesn't. So, while some of us like to be tickled, other people don't. And although some people like it when a friend leans against them really close, this makes some people uncomfortable. We all have the right for people to respect our personal space and boundaries and to refuse to consent to things that cross those lines. For example, do you like to be tickled? But do people sometimes tickle you for longer than you'd like? You don't have to let anyone touch you if you don't want them to. Likewise, you should never be forced to hug, touch or kiss anybody, for any reason, if you don't want to. Whoever the person is, and no matter how close you are, if something makes you feel uncomfortable, then you don't have to do it.

"Hanging out with someone isn't like watching Netflix, where the programme picks up exactly where you left off. In real life, you have the right to change your mind about what you want – even if you've 'gone farther' before – you can take things slow, rewind, even change programs."

Chella Quint, Period Positive

'No' and 'Stop' are important words and should always be respected, whoever is saying them. Some people find it easy to say no. Others may feel embarrassed, or afraid to speak up for themselves. It can be especially hard to say no to adults because we're brought up to respect people in authority and to do as they tell us. But you absolutely have the right to say 'no' to something like a hug with anyone, even if it's with an adult you care about, and who you've hugged lots of times before.

Being assertive is a skill you can learn, just like riding a bike or baking a cake. You can practise saying no and refusing consent. So, if someone asks for a hug, and you don't want to, try to say 'No thanks' or 'I don't want to', calmly and clearly. You could move away from them.

If you want to, try telling the person how you feel and ask them to do something else instead. So, someone who prefers not to be hugged might say: 'I feel trapped when you put your arms around me tightly, and I don't like it. Can we just hold hands instead?' If someone acts hurt when you ask them to stop doing something, you just need to say 'No' again and reiterate how you feel. You could say: 'I understand you mean well but it makes me feel uncomfortable.'

Of course, there may be times when you want to say yes, or show you are happy to be hugged. You can show your consent by smiling and hugging someone back so that person knows you're consenting to and enjoying the contact.

How to SAY NO

THINK ABOUT

What are your personal boundaries?

What would you say to someone if they were making you uncomfortable?

CHANGING *your mind*

Consent can also be withdrawn at any time. If two friends are mucking about and play-fighting and suddenly one has had enough and says stop, the game should stop. It doesn't matter that the person wanted to play the game when it started or that they were enjoying the game up until that moment. It doesn't matter that the other people who were playing the game might be disappointed. As soon as one person changes their mind about playing and the game stops being fun for them, they can ask to stop and everyone else who's involved should respect their wishes.

This holds true for any situation where your personal space and boundaries are in question. Yes can become no at any point. As soon as something starts to make you feel uncomfortable or unhappy, you can and should stop it.

When it comes to personal boundaries and protecting your personal space, you have the right to say no to any kind of touching if it makes you feel uncomfortable.

THINK ABOUT

Have you ever tried to make someone do something they didn't want to do? How do you think this made them feel?

Have you ever changed your mind part-way through doing something and decided you wanted to stop? Did you express your feelings?

Consent is not for ever or for everything

Imagine that a friend asks if they can have one of your crisps and you say yes. Then you go to get a drink and when you come back you find that they have eaten all of the rest of your lunch too. They've crossed a line! Saying yes to giving them one crisp was not the same as agreeing they could eat all your sandwiches. The same principle applies to consent, too. Consenting to one form of physical contact does not automatically mean that a person has consented to other types of physical contact. So, consenting to a hug does not mean that a person has also consented to a kiss. And when a person lets someone put an arm around them, it does not mean that they consent to being touched elsewhere.

It doesn't matter if you are at home, at a friend's house, at school, in the playground, or on a date — wherever you are and whatever you're doing, the rules about consent still apply. You're in control of your body and the most important thing is how you feel. This is especially important when it comes to your private parts. Even parents and doctors should ask before touching you in places usually covered by your underwear, and you always have the right to say no if it makes you feel uncomfortable.

Talking PANTS

The NSPCC came up with the word PANTS to remind kids of what they call the underwear rule: your underwear covers your privates for a reason.

Privates are private.

Always remember your body belongs to you.

No means no.

Talk about secrets that upset you.

Speak up, someone can help.

From the NSPCC's 'Talking Pants' campaign

Consent
and
DISABILITY

The law defines disability as a physical or mental impairment that has a 'substantial' and 'long-term' negative effect on your ability to do normal daily activities. This includes physical disabilities, such as being blind or deaf, and mental disabilities such as long-term depression or dementia. Some disabilities are clearly visible: for example, using a wheelchair to get around signals to other people that the wheelchair user is disabled. However, not all disabilities are visible. Many mental disabilities, and some types of physical disability, can't be seen by looking at a person. We should never judge whether a person has a disability just by looking at them.

Having a disability can influence a person's personal boundaries. For example, some disabilities might mean that a person experiences high levels of discomfort when touched. Most people probably wouldn't mind being hugged by a close friend. However, for a disabled person who experiences higher levels of pain, being hugged could really hurt. If we always ask before touching people, we can avoid causing unnecessary pain. Never assume that a person's personal boundaries are based on your own or other people's. Everyone's boundaries are different, so always ask first.

> *Never assume that a person's personal boundaries are based on your own or other people's. Everyone's boundaries are different, so always ask first.*

Depending on a person's illness or disability, they might have to see a doctor or healthcare professional regularly. In many cases this can be really helpful, for example if somebody has anorexia, depression, or another type of mental illness, they can be looked after and supported to get better. Some disabled people also have a carer – someone who looks after them and supports them in their day-to-day lives. Doctors and carers often have physical contact with a disabled person, and that takes a great level of trust. However, it is important to remember that you still always have consent over what does and doesn't happen to your own body. If a doctor or carer wants to touch you and you refuse, this is your right just as it would be if it was any other person who wanted to make physical contact with you. Similarly, it is your choice what drugs you do or don't put into your body, what treatment you decide to have, and what kind of support you want from other people.

The only time someone's medical choices can be made by another person on their behalf is when the law rules that they don't have the capacity to make choices for themselves. 'Capacity' means the ability to understand and use information to make a decision, and then to communicate any decision made. For some people with severe mental illnesses or learning difficulties, decisions are made in their best interests by the health professionals treating them. A person's capacity to make their own choices can change so should always be assessed at the time that consent is required.

my views on CONSENT

Zara Todd

ZARA TODD is a youth worker and women's and disability rights campaigner. She runs workshops with young people about consent and disability.

ON PERSONAL BOUNDARIES AND *disability*

Boundaries are very personal to an individual. Everybody needs to figure out what their own boundaries are, and also respect that other people's personal boundaries will be different to their own. For example, for most people they would feel comfortable for someone to tap them on the shoulder. But some people might have a condition that means that being tapped on the shoulder could cause pain or make them feel uncomfortable. They might wear shoulder pads to lessen their chance of being hurt by other people. However, if everyone just asked first, it would make this person's life a lot easier. Part of the way that you respect someone is by giving them control over themselves, so respect their personal boundaries, and always ask before you interact with someone.

THINK ABOUT

Have you ever made assumptions about whether someone is disabled or not just by looking at them?

Is it ever okay to touch someone without their consent?

WHY ARE PEOPLE'S IDEAS ABOUT PERSONAL SPACE *different?*

What is personal to me is likely to have a much lower threshold than what is personal to a non-disabled person. People have been allowed into my personal space for years, for example when I have physiotherapy, which makes my body feel a lot better. But this has made my understanding of personal space very different to other people's.

IT'S NEVER *your fault*

You know your body better than anyone else. If someone's doing something that makes you uncomfortable, then make sure you tell them, because most people aren't mind readers. If somebody says 'I'm going to do this' and you know it's going to hurt, you have a right to say 'I don't want you to do that'. If you tell them and they don't stop, remember it's not your fault if they don't listen to you. You haven't done anything wrong – never blame yourself if somebody else isn't respecting your boundaries.

Is it weird to dislike something that everybody else seems to be okay with?

We're all individuals, and how we like to interact with people is different for every person. You're not weird or strange for not wanting things to happen to you, whatever that might be. Never feel like you can't say what you need or want because people might think you're weird or strange.

Under PRESSURE

There is a big difference between consenting to do something because you really want to, and doing something because someone has made you do it. It's important to be able to know when it's right to consent to something and when it's not, and it's especially important not to pressure other people into doing things they don't want to do.

All of us are surrounded by people who try to influence what we do. Much of the time, most of us are happy to have this kind of pressure because these influences are positive, like when a friend persuades us to join a club with them or a parent encourages us to try a new hobby.

But sometimes, people can put pressure on us to consent to something that is not good for us. They might pressurise someone to skip school for a day, smoke a cigarette or take something from a shop without paying for it. These kinds of choices and decisions can have serious and damaging consequences and, as you grow older, you will be faced with other challenging choices. Sometimes the right answer won't always be clear. We have to try to learn how to make the right decisions for ourselves and refuse to let pressure make us consent to things that are bad for us.

❝ *We have to try to learn how to make the right decisions for ourselves and refuse to let pressure make us consent to things that are bad for us.* **❞**

TRUST YOUR *gut*

Sometimes we may not feel certain if something is wrong or not, but we know it makes us feel weird, scared, or uncomfortable. If something feels wrong, it is most likely to be wrong for you. No one has the right to make you feel that way. If a person or situation makes you feel uncomfortable in any way, speak up or leave. You know what is right for you, no matter what anyone else says or tries to make you feel. If something doesn't feel right, it isn't right.

How pressure works

Pressure works in different ways. Some types of pressure are more obvious than others. For example, someone might threaten to hurt another person if they don't do something, or threaten to spread rumours about them if they refuse to consent to something. However, most of the time pressure happens in subtler ways. Have you ever done something risky just because others were doing it? Some people give into pressure as a way to fit in and be accepted by a certain group of people. So when someone wants them to try cigarettes and says everyone else is doing it, they consent because they don't want to be left out, or for people to make fun of them.

Some people put pressure on others by playing with their emotions. They try to get their own way by acting hurt and by making the other person feel silly or bad for saying 'no'. All kinds of pressure are designed to influence people to consent to something they'd rather not do.

THINK ABOUT

Has someone ever persuaded you to do something you knew was wrong? How did it feel?

Being aware
OF YOUR OWN
PRESSURE

We are all capable of putting pressure on other people, or trying to influence others to do things they might not want to do. This isn't always a bad thing. For example, a doctor might try to convince someone to get stitches even though it will be painful because it's in their best interest. You might try to convince your friend to do their homework on time because they will get in trouble if they hand it in late. Using our power to influence others can be a good thing if we are trying to get people to do what's best for them.

However, sometimes people don't want to do what we feel is in their best interest. They might be too scared or they might feel that something else is a better option for them. We don't always have to agree with someone's choices, but it's important to

THINK ABOUT

What do you think about a person who tries to get a friend to do stuff they don't want to do?

respect that their choices are their own. Part of being a good friend is supporting someone to make their own decisions and accepting that we might not always agree, and that's okay.

Sometimes we can put pressure on other people when it isn't in their best interest. This could be because what we're trying to do is in our best interest, or because we think it will be right for them, but actually we've misjudged the situation. We all put negative pressure on to others sometimes and it's important that we recognise when we're doing it, think about how the other person must be feeling, and stop if it's making them upset.

Sometimes someone might say 'yes' to you even when they mean no. Learning to be sensitive to other people's emotions can take time. Before we interact with anyone else, we should always try to find out if they're giving enthusiastic consent. Remember to think about their best interests, and respect their right not to consent.

Have you ever pressured someone into doing something they didn't want to? How will you act differently next time?

my views on
CONSENT

Alice Pinney

ALICE PINNEY is a proud GirlGuiding Advocate. She believes it's important to always be nice.

WHY IS IT IMPORTANT TO TALK ABOUT *consent?*

I don't think consent is taught well in most schools. The word 'consent' was never brought up in any of my PSHE lessons. For me, it was one of those words I just picked up as I grew older, but I was never explicitly told by anyone what consent means. I think we all learn about it, but we don't always learn about it in the correct way, and we're not all given the same definition.

ON THE ROLE OF *social media*

I think the problem is that there's a lot of bombardment about this word consent – what it is and what it means. What we see on the TV or social media isn't necessarily always right. It's quite easy to be affected by what you see and hear and not develop your own opinion and your own personal boundaries. By educating ourselves and others about consent, we develop the tools and understanding to make decisions for ourselves.

"By educating ourselves and others about consent, we develop the tools and understanding to make decisions for ourselves."

NEGATIVE INFLUENCES *online*

There's so much pressure on young people to be more grown up. My nine-year-old sister's on Instagram, which wasn't even around when I was nine years old. I feel like young people now are seeing a constant bombardment of what the perfect image is, or the perfect relationship. We're constantly exposed to ideas and images about what we're expected to be. In many ways social media is taking away our right to choose what we want for ourselves.

ON *sharing* ONLINE CONTENT

Whenever you share a picture or message online, make sure you have permission from whoever sent it to you first. It's an invasion of privacy to share personal pictures or messages around. Even if you share something with one person, they could pass it on to someone else, and this can be really devastating for the person who sent the photo or the message in the first place. It can also have such a negative impact on mental health if someone's privacy is invaded and their trust is broken.

A lot of the time consent is about power. If somebody shares a picture of someone without their consent, they are taking power out of their hands. They are taking away their ability to choose what is and isn't shared about them.

 ## *Online tips:*

Social media can be quite difficult to navigate. I would say sometimes the best thing for people is to just not have it. Most people do have an online presence now though, and you might choose to sign up to one in the future. So here are some things I've learnt about staying safe online:

Check your privacy settings. Always read the small print when you sign up to a website. Make sure your posts can only be seen by people you know and trust.

Always be nice. Don't share pictures without people's permission, or write nasty comments. This way you can do your bit to help other people to stay safe online.

Make sure you always know who you're talking to online. If someone gets in touch with you who you don't know in real life, it's best to ignore them. If they keep bothering you, block and report them.

Don't judge. Try not to judge people on one picture or one post, without knowing anything about them. This way online space can be nicer for everyone.

Types of
CONSENT

We can give or refuse consent in a whole range of situations, but some can have more impact on our lives than others. Here we're going to look at the importance of online consent, sexual consent and medical consent.

Online consent

A lot of our lives are spent online. We use the Internet for school, work and to talk to friends. We can use it to play games and write blogs and lots of other positive things. Sometimes however, using the Internet can make people feel worried or upset. They might come across things they don't want to see. They may get mean comments or abuse when they're playing a game online. Some people have their social media pages hacked into, their profiles changed either for fun or by someone who is bullying them, or someone may post nasty comments in their name. This can happen if they leave their computer or mobile device on unattended without logging off a site. There is also the risk that people they

'meet' online may want to hurt them and are pretending they are someone else to become their 'friend'.

This all sounds scary, and it is, but you can prevent it. In order to stop people accessing or sharing your information and details without your consent, it's vital to learn how to use privacy settings and how to use passwords and other login details safely. Ask for help to make sure profiles are not public and available for anyone to see. If something happens online that you don't like, find out how to block that contact and tell a trusted adult immediately. Most sites also have a report button which you can use to send any comments to the site to investigate.

"*There is also the risk that people they 'meet' online may want to hurt them and are pretending they are someone else to become their 'friend'.***"**

Be SMART

Follow the SMART rules to be safe online.

Safety: Never give personal information away online. Only use nicknames as usernames, never your real full name.

Meeting: Never meet up with people that you meet online, without your family. They are still strangers even if you have been talking to them for a long time.

Accepting: Be careful when accepting files from strangers. They may contain viruses, images or other things that make us feel uncomfortable or worried.

Reliable: Someone online might lie about who they are and information on the Internet may not be true. Always check information with other websites, books or someone who knows. If you like chatting online it's best to only chat to your real-world friends and family.

Tell: Tell your parent, carer or a trusted adult if someone or something makes you feel uncomfortable or worried, or if you or someone you know is being bullied online.

Sexual CONSENT

As you grow up, you might be attracted to someone, and want to be more than just friends. If they like you too, you might start to date. When we care about people it's natural to want to show them affection, for example by kissing them, but it's really important to make sure that both partners consent to any physical contact they have.

There are lots of ways to show affection, such as hugging, cuddling and kissing, which can be great if these are things you both want to do, feel ready for and freely consent to. A couple might want to touch each other in a sexual way, for example by touching the breasts, vagina or penis. Sometimes one partner might ask the other to take some of their clothes off and take photos of themselves. The important thing to remember is that if either person feels uncomfortable or unhappy, then both people should stop immediately.

It's really important to say no if you think things are going too far or to stop if you think your partner is unhappy or uncomfortable in any way. Remember, your body is your own and you don't have to consent to anything that doesn't feel right. Treat other people's bodies the same way you want them to treat yours: with respect and kindness, remembering that their body belongs to them and it's their right to decide what happens to it.

It seems people really have a problem understanding that before you have sex with someone, and that's every time you have sex with them, make sure they want to have sex with you. This goes for men, women, everyone. Whoever you are initiating sexytimes with, just make sure they are actually genuinely up for it. That's it. It's not hard. Really.

Emmeline May, sexual consent campaigner

Getting CONSENT

By law, adults have a responsibility to make sure their sexual partners are agreeing to have sex. This means that a person is actively agreeing to have sex with another person. Consent must be given by both partners each and every time a couple has sex. Even if both partners give consent at first, either partner has the right to change their mind at any point. If someone seems at all hesitant or uncomfortable in any way, it is not consent. If someone is particularly vulnerable, for example if they are too young, asleep, very drunk or unconscious, they are not legally capable of providing consent, and sex with them is by default sexual assault, even if they give active consent.

THINK ABOUT

What do you think about a person who tries to make their partner do more than they feel happy with?

What does it say about how much that person cares about their partner's feelings?

Medical CONSENT

Let's say you visit your doctor for a medical check-up. Even if you're under 16 and with a parent, the doctor should talk directly to you. They should ask you questions about your health and tell you what tests they plan to do that day. If they want to do something like listen to your heartbeat, they should ask for your permission to do so. Medical consent is an important type of consent and applies to us all, regardless of what treatment we need.

By law, doctors and nurses must ask a patient for their consent before giving any type of medical treatment, from a blood test to major surgery. Before a doctor can perform an operation, they should talk to the patient about the surgery – why it is necessary and what it involves – and make sure it is what the patient wants. If the patient is able to understand what is involved and gives their consent, then the procedure goes ahead.

People aged 16 or over are entitled to consent to their own treatment, and this can only be overruled in exceptional circumstances. While children under 16 are not automatically assumed to be capable of making decisions about their medical treatment, they can consent if they're believed to have enough intelligence, competence and understanding to fully appreciate what's involved. However, they usually make this decision with their parents or the people who have parental responsibility for them.

Do you think it's fair that young people under the age of 16 have a say in their medical treatment? Why? When might it be a problem?

FGM

You may have heard about FGM in the news. FGM stands for Female Genital Mutilation and is sometimes called being 'cut'. It is a procedure in which parts or all of the external female genitals are removed. Some people claim FGM is done for medical reasons but there are no medical reasons to carry out FGM. In many countries, including the UK, FGM is illegal.

FGM is often carried out on girls as young as one. Girls of this age are neither informed nor old enough to consent to the operation. Even when girls are older, it is hard to determine whether they can give free and informed consent, because they rarely know all the facts and risks, and because of the pressure put on them to have the procedure by their family and community.

FGM leaves girls and women with serious health and emotional problems. If you or someone you know is at risk or has undergone FGM you should tell a teacher or a school nurse. Any concerns will be treated confidentially and referred to someone who can help. Professionals can give families advice and information to help them understand it is against the law and not in the best interests of their daughter.

> *Most people in Eritrea think that if a girl is cut, she will grow up to be a good girl – that she will not bring shame on her family and she will marry well. If a girl is not cut, they think she will grow up to be a 'slut' – a girl who thinks about sex and will not be satisfied by one man. Most people feel this way in my country and it is only those who are educated that disagree with cutting.*

Hadas, as quoted on the NSPCC and Childline websites
www.childline.org.uk/get-involved/real-life-stories/fgm-hadas-story/

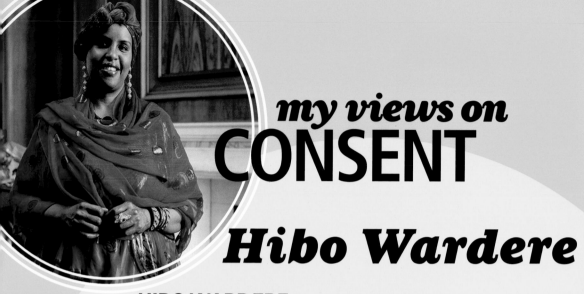

my views on
CONSENT

Hibo Wardere

HIBO WARDERE is an anti-FGM campaigner who loves to wear colourful outfits. She experienced FGM when she was younger, and now she goes into schools to talk about it.

WHAT HAS **FGM** GOT TO DO WITH *consent?*

I'm very proud of my community. It has many beautiful things about it. However FGM is one part of my community that I didn't chose to be a part of. Even though I didn't choose it, I had it done to me anyway. Most people who have FGM done to them don't have a choice.

FGM is usually done to people when they are too young to understand what is happening. Or it can be done when people are older, but it is almost always done without the consent of the person it is being done to. If people knew what FGM was, they wouldn't want it to happen to them. FGM takes away the right to say yes or no.

Consent is vital for all of us. If we don't respect people's right to consent, we allow FGM to keep happening, and to keep hurting people.

WHY IS FGM SO BAD?

When someone performs FGM, they take away a part of a girl's body without her consent. I believe it's important for people to have every part of their body intact. Every part of a person's body is beautiful. Some people think that FGM is necessary. I would say to them: 'Why does she need to have anything cut off of her? She is perfect the way she is.'

THE *effects* OF FGM

FGM is very painful. When it is first done, it causes a lot of blood loss and depending on the equipment used, can also cause infections.

It can lead to lots of long-term problems that last into adult life. These include long-term pain, infections, bleeding, trouble going to the toilet, difficulty having sex, depression and other mental health problems. In some cases it can even lead to infertility and difficulties during childbirth.

FGM has many physical consequences, but it has emotional consequences too. It can make people feel unhappy and unloved. FGM is sometimes said to be done for 'medical' reasons, but it has no health benefits and no positive effects.

> **" If people knew what FGM was, they wouldn't want it to happen to them. "**

What should somebody do if they are worried about FGM?

If anything has scared you, there's a reason for that. If anything has made you feel uncomfortable, there's a reason for that. It's your brain telling you to go and get some help and talk to somebody you trust.

Some people think FGM only happens in other countries, but FGM happens in the UK too. FGM is a type of child abuse, and child abuse does not have colour, race, religion or country. If you're worried about FGM, talk to someone you trust.

Consent and
THE LAW

In the UK there are laws about consent. People who break these laws can be punished.

Online

Anyone who makes threats to you on the Internet could be committing a criminal offence. It's against the law in the UK to use the phone system or Internet to cause alarm or distress. If threats are made against someone they should make a complaint to the police.

SEXUAL CONSENT

It is an offence for anyone to have any sexual activity with a person under the age of 16.

You may know the term 'age of consent'. This is about sexual consent, and means the age at which a young person can legally consent to sexual activity. Under the age of 16, they cannot consent, and it is an offence for anyone to have any sexual activity with them. At the age of 16, a young person can legally consent – or not.

It is an offence for a person aged 18 or over to have any sexual activity with a person under the age of 18 if the older person holds a position of trust (for example a teacher or social worker). Such sexual activity is an abuse of the position of trust.

It is an offence to take an indecent photograph of a child under the age of 16 or to involve a child under 16 in a photograph that is itself indecent even if the child's role is not.

Medical Consent

For consent to be valid, it must be given voluntarily by an appropriately informed person who has the capacity to consent. This is known as being 'Gillick competent'. In cases where a young person or child deemed 'Gillick competent' refuses to consent to treatment, a court can overrule their decision if this could lead to death or severe permanent injury. If a child under 16 doesn't have the capacity to consent to treatment, someone with parental responsibility can consent for them.

FGM

In some countries, for example The Gambia, FGM can be punishable with up to lifetime imprisonment. In the UK, the FGM Act (2003) makes it illegal to help, support or arrange for FGM to be performed on a girl either in the UK or abroad. The offence can be punished by up to 14 years in prison, a fine, or both. In 2015, the UK government introduced a new law requiring certain professionals to report known cases of FGM in under-18s to the police.

❝There is no trust more sacred than the one the world holds with children. There is no duty more important than ensuring that their rights are respected, that their welfare is protected, that their lives are free from fear and want and that they can grow up in peace.❞

Kofi Annan, Secretary-General of the United Nations 1997–2006.

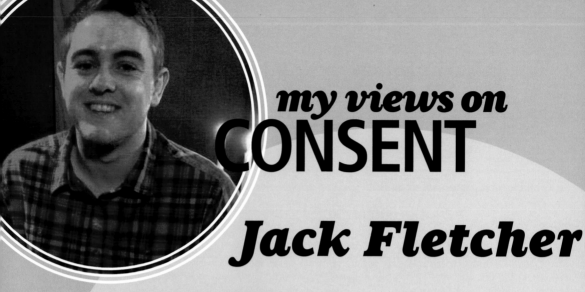

my views on
CONSENT

Jack Fletcher

JACK FLETCHER is a junior doctor. He has also worked for Sexpression, going into schools to talk about puberty, sex and healthy relationships.

CAN YOU EXPLAIN A BIT MORE ABOUT WHAT

'Gillick competence' is?

The Gillick competence is an assumption that children under 16 can give consent if they're able to prove it. Usually in medicine it's assumed that an adult can give consent, and it must always be given in verbal or written capacity, or physically. Like if someone gives you their arm, it's assumed that it's okay to take their blood – unless it's life or death, I'm not just going to run over to someone and stab them with a needle! I always ask for consent first. But with children, because of the law saying they are their parent/carers' responsibility until 16, there's a grey area over whether or not they can make their own medical choices. Because of the Gillick competence, children are given the benefit of the doubt that they're able to make the best decision for themselves. If they're able to relay that information and understand what's going on and come up with a reasonable decision based on what they've been told, that displays capacity and understanding. So they're considered able to make that decision for themselves.

WHAT IF THE PARENT/CARER REFUSES
to give consent?

Let's say a parent or carer refuses to give consent for their child to have an operation. This is very rare, but can sometimes happen, for example if the children's family are Jehovah's Witnesses. If the doctor feels like this operation is in the child's best interest, they can apply to a court of law to get permission to do it.

Medical consent is different to other types of consent

"I'm not just going to run over to someone and stab them with a needle!"

The general rule for consent is if something is making you feel uncomfortable you should ask the other person to stop. However, when you go to see a doctor, lots of things you experience might be outside of your normal comfort zone. For example, the doctor might examine different parts of your body under your clothes and this could feel a bit awkward. Another example is that nobody likes having a needle stuck in their arm to have their blood taken. This can be unpleasant and sometimes even a little bit painful (even though it's a lot less painful than you would imagine!).

Although medical practices can sometimes be uncomfortable or unpleasant at the time, we often choose to consent to them because they are in our best interests. Doctors are only looking to help us and they give advice on what's best for us so that we can feel more comfortable, healthy and happy in the long run. Trust your doctor, and if you are feeling really scared or uncomfortable about anything, talk to them about your concerns. Doctors are all trained in consent, and they are there to look after you and make you feel as informed and comfortable as possible.

What if I didn't CONSENT?

Sometimes people can abuse our right to consent. For example, someone might always keep trying to hug you, even when you've repeatedly asked them to stop. Nobody ever has the right to do anything with or to you without your enthusiastic consent. If they do, then you have every right to tell them to stop, and to tell someone what has happened to try to stop it from happening again.

Sexual abuse is when someone forces sexual contact on someone without their consent. A person is sexually abused when they are persuaded or forced to take part in any sexual activities, whether or not there is physical contact. It is abuse whether the victim is able to say no or has been coerced into doing something that makes them feel uncomfortable or hurts them. So, it is sexual abuse if an abuser touches or forces a child to touch them in a sexual way, or even if the abuser shows them pornographic images or makes them have a sexual conversation by text or online.

This kind of abuse is shocking but sadly around one in 20 children in the UK have been sexually abused. The impacts can be devastating. People who have been abused may have trouble eating or sleeping. They may feel angry, scared, depressed and cut off from friends and family. They may suffer from depression, anxiety and many other problems into adulthood.

DEALING WITH *abuse*

The important thing to remember is that if someone is abused it is not their fault or the result of anything they may or may not have done. The abuse happened without their full voluntary and informed consent. They are never to blame for the abuse. Abusers sometimes threaten victims to stop them speaking out because they know they have committed a crime and could get into real trouble. Secrecy only helps the abuser. If someone is being abused, they should report it immediately to someone they trust, such as a parent, carer, teacher, a friend's parent, a doctor, or the police. They can also call a helpline such as Childline on 0800 1111.

It can be even harder for a victim to report abuse if the abuser is someone they know or is a family member who they may care for or who has otherwise treated them well. The abuse must still be reported, to help the victim, the other people who may be hurt by the abuser and the abuser themselves.

People who have been abused usually need some help recovering from it. When someone has a broken leg they see a doctor. When someone has an emotional injury they see a therapist or counsellors, who help people to work through issues like this. Talking to a trained professional can be easier than talking to friends and family and although they don't tell people what to do, counsellors and therapists can help people find ways to help themselves too.

> *" You can recognise survivors of abuse by their courage. When silence is so very inviting, they step forward and share their truth so others know they aren't alone. "*
>
> Jeanne McElvaney, **Healing Insights: Effects of Abuse for Adults Abused as Children**

What do you THINK ?

Now that you've read this book, what do you think about consent? What are some of the most important issues and problems to do with the idea of consent?

Here are some of the questions we've raised:

? INTRODUCING CONSENT

When have you heard the word consent before? How was it used? What would you like to know about it?

? WHAT IS CONSENT?

What do you think when you hear the word consent?

Why do you think some people are confused by consent?

What do people mean by enthusiastic consent?

? RECOGNISING CONSENT

How does being able to understand different types of body language help us to recognise when consent is being given and when it is being refused?

If someone doesn't say no, does that mean they give consent?

If someone goes quiet when you ask them to do something, does that mean they agree to do it?

? YOUR BODY, YOUR CHOICE

Why is it important to respect people's personal boundaries?

Why does everyone need to learn how to be assertive?

Is it OK to change your mind and refuse consent after you've already given it?

Is it ever okay to do something to someone when they haven't consented?

? UNDER PRESSURE

Is pressure to consent to something always a bad thing?

What would you say to someone who always tries to make their friends do things they don't want to?

If something feels wrong, does that mean it is wrong?

? TYPES OF CONSENT

What are the SMART rules about online consent?

Why is medical consent only given by people who can understand the information given to them about a medical procedure?

Does being in a relationship mean your partner automatically consents to what you want to do?

Thinking about Consent

You've thought about a lot of questions throughout the book, but here are a few final big ones to consider ...

Why do you think it's important to keep talking about some of the trickier or more awkward aspects of consent, such as sexual consent? How do you think talking about consent could change the way some people behave? If you could plan a lesson to be taught in schools about consent, what would you say?

? WHAT TO DO WHEN CONSENT IS ABUSED

If someone consents to something, can it be termed abuse?

How should people deal with abuse?

What can we DO?

Now that you understand what consent means and how important it is, you can help to spread the word. One way to do this is in the way you behave and the way you react to other people. You can feel more confident to say no to someone when they are trying to persuade you to consent to something you don't want to do. You can think more about whether other people are consenting or not. You can stand up for others when you can see they are too afraid to stand up for themselves.

We can all make a difference simply by talking about consent too. You could discuss it with friends and family, or with your teachers at school. Perhaps you could encourage your school to hold a talk about consent. The more people think and talk about consent, the more people will be empowered to say what they really feel and want and the more people will understand when yes really means yes and when it's more complicated than that!

Useful information

If you would like to know more about consent, take a look at these websites.

Childline workers are ready to help with any problems www.childline.org.uk/ Telephone 0800 1111 (calls are free)

The NSPCC's 'Talking Pants' campaign www.nspcc.org.uk/preventing-abuse/ keeping-children-safe/underwear-rule/

The NHS rules about medical consent for children ww.nhs.uk/conditions/consent-to-treatment/children/

GLOSSARY

abuse to treat with cruelty or violence, especially regularly or repeatedly

anorexia an eating disorder that causes people to stop eating

assertive having or showing a confident and forceful personality

body language expressing feelings with gestures or body posture

campaigner a person who takes part in a project to change something important

capacity when someone is able to understand the information given to them

communication expressing ideas and feelings or giving people information

dementia a brain condition in which people (usually older people) suffer from symptoms including memory loss, having problems recognising people they know and being unsure about where they are

gender being male or female

indecent improper, offensive or shocking

informed to know what the benefits and risks of a decision are

initiator person who starts or begins something

medical consent giving consent for a medical procedure such as an operation

negotiate work out an arrangement or solution that suits both sides

personal boundaries the limits to what a person feels comfortable with when it comes to people being close to or touching them

physiotherapy physical treatment such as massage or exercise rather than medicine or surgery

pressurise to cajole, persuade or force someone to do something

sexual assault having sexual contact with someone who is unwilling or unable to give their full, enthusiastic consent

sexual consent when a person who is free and able to make their own decision willingly agrees to have sex or engage in a sexual activity with someone

voluntary when someone does something willingly and by choice

Index